This is the Spirit of Revelation

 Published 2019
Printed in the United States of America

22 21 20 19 1 2 3 4

ISBN: 978-1-7336585-2-2

The paper used in this publication meets the minimum requirements of the American National Standard for Information Sciences–Permanence of Paper for Printed Library Materials, ANSI Z39.48-1992.

For great resources and information, follow us:

Facebook: www.facebook.com/lds.eduempowerkids
Instagram: @dina_empower_ldskids
Website: empowerlatterdaysaintkids.org

Thank you to the following individuals for their research, support, and editing during this project:
Jenny Webb, MA and Melody Bergman

Check out the glossary at the end of the book to find definitions to important words.

This is the Spirit of Revelation

By Dina Alexander, MS
Design & Illustration by Jera Mehrdad

LIFE IS FULL OF MYSTERIES.
AND
"TO THOSE WHO HAVE
EYES TO SEE
AND EARS TO HEAR,
IT IS CLEAR THAT THE
FATHER AND THE SON ARE
GIVING AWAY THE SECRETS
OF THE UNIVERSE!"

—Neal A. Maxwell

God loves you
and wants to speak to you.
He wants to hear
from you too!

So,
He gave us
personal revelation.

"IF WE ARE TO
HAVE ANY HOPE OF
SIFTING THROUGH THE MYRIAD
OF VOICES AND
THE PHILOSOPHIES
OF MEN THAT
ATTACK TRUTH,
WE MUST LEARN TO
RECEIVE REVELATION."

—Russell M. Nelson

Revelation is:
Communication from God to His children.

Heavenly Father can speak to us and answer our questions in many ways. He uses the Holy Ghost to communicate with us.

CHOICES of the DAY

What SHOULD I EAT?

Candy? VEGGIES?

CHIPS!?

MAYBE SOMEthing SALTY AND Sweet! = Apples & Peanut Butter!

BE Nice or MEAN?

READ OR WATCH TV

Play VIDEO GAMES or soccer

STAY UP LATE OR go to BED EARLY

Jogging PANTS? or JEANS?

WHAT SHOULD I WEAR?

DRess or SKIRT?

STRIPED or SOLID?

THAT LOOKS DUMB

UGGG!

PJs TO SCHOOL is cool, right?

There are so many voices and choices around us.

We need our Heavenly Father's guidance to find truth and to learn how to be happy.

Sometimes you will feel prompted to act.

"...WE MANY TIMES RECEIVE REVELATION WITHOUT RECOGNIZING PRECISELY HOW OR WHEN WE ARE RECEIVING REVELATION.... SOMETIMES THE SPIRIT OF REVELATION WILL OPERATE IMMEDIATELY AND INTENSELY, OTHER TIMES SUBTLY AND GRADUALLY, AND OFTEN SO DELICATELY YOU MAY NOT EVEN CONSCIOUSLY RECOGNIZE IT."

—David A. Bednar

STAND UP
FOR YOUR
friend

Many times, you will have a thought or words come into your mind. Later you may realize that you were inspired by the Holy Ghost to act.

But more often, you will have questions and you will seek for answers.

There are many smart ways we can find answers.
And there are many trustworthy places where we can find answers.

You can ask your loved ones.
You can search the scriptures.

You can listen to the words of prophets, both past prophets and living prophets.

And of course,
you can pray!

"And as all have not faith, seek ye diligently and teach one another words of wisdom; yea, seek ye out of the best books words of wisdom; seek learning, even by study and also by faith."

—Doctrine and Covenants 88:118

PREPARING

"THE ABILITY TO QUALIFY FOR, RECEIVE, AND ACT ON PERSONAL REVELATION IS THE SINGLE MOST IMPORTANT SKILL THAT CAN BE ACQUIRED IN THIS LIFE."

—Julie B. Beck

Usually, getting answers requires more than just asking.

We can invite and keep the Holy Ghost in our lives so that we can hear His promptings, inspiration, warnings, and peaceful nudgings.

You can do many things to prepare to receive personal revelation.

You can live kindly.

You can listen to good music.

You can study the scriptures.

TAKING A BREAK FROM SOCIAL MEDIA
See Ya In A Week!

You can fast from food
or technology.

You can use honest
and reliable sources to
research your question.

You can ask a worthy
priesthood holder for a
priesthood blessing.

To hear the Holy Ghost,
we need to listen.

You can prepare to listen
by going to a quiet place.

Take time to listen to your feelings and any impressions or words that the Holy Ghost may communicate to you.

Preparation is important. In Doctrine and Covenants 38:30, God reminded Joseph Smith that "if ye are prepared ye shall not fear." When we prepare, we can be ready for anything!

"IN COMING DAYS, IT WILL NOT BE POSSIBLE TO SURVIVE SPIRITUALLY WITHOUT THE GUIDING, DIRECTING, COMFORTING, AND CONSTANT INFLUENCE OF THE HOLY GHOST.... IF WE ARE TO HAVE ANY HOPE OF SIFTING THROUGH THE MYRIAD OF VOICES AND THE PHILOSOPHIES OF MEN THAT ATTACK TRUTH, WE MUST LEARN TO RECEIVE REVELATION."

—Russell M. Nelson

You can use your own voice and pray to your Father in Heaven.

Remember, He loves you and wants to hear from you.

"... OUR SMALL AND SIMPLE CHOICE TO PRAY ALLOWS GOD TO UNLOCK THE POWERS OF HEAVEN IN OUR BEHALF. THE HOLY GHOST IS FREE TO FILL OUR MINDS AND HEARTS, LEADING US TOWARDS HIM AND OUR ETERNAL DESTINY. I CAN THINK OF NO GREATER THING."

—Virginia H. Pearce

He wants to know
your plans, your hopes,
your questions, and
your fears.

Spend time talking
with God!

Don't just give Him a list of your wants and stop the discussion. Share your thoughts and then take the time to listen.

If more thoughts arrive while you are listening, talk about them as well. In a conversation, both sides take turns.

"The most important thing you can do is to learn to talk to God.
Talk to Him as you would talk to your father, for He is your Father, and He wants you to talk to Him. He wants you to cultivate ears to listen, when He gives you the impressions of the Spirit to tell you what to do."

—President Harold B. Lee

When we ask,
we need to have real intent.

We must ask in faith,
meaning that we believe
that God loves us
and will answer us.

"AND WHEN YE SHALL RECEIVE THESE THINGS, I WOULD EXHORT YOU THAT YE WOULD ASK GOD, THE ETERNAL FATHER, IN THE NAME OF CHRIST, IF THESE THINGS ARE NOT TRUE; AND IF YE SHALL ASK WITH A SINCERE HEART, WITH REAL INTENT, HAVING FAITH IN CHRIST, HE WILL MANIFEST THE TRUTH OF IT UNTO YOU, BY THE POWER OF THE HOLY GHOST. AND BY THE POWER OF THE HOLY GHOST YE MAY KNOW THE TRUTH OF ALL THINGS."

—Moroni 10:4–5

LISTENING and getting ANSWERS

"PERHAPS THE SINGLE GREATEST THING I LEARNED FROM READING THE BOOK OF MORMON IS THAT THE VOICE OF THE SPIRIT COMES AS A FEELING RATHER THAN A SOUND. YOU WILL LEARN, AS I HAVE LEARNED, TO 'LISTEN' FOR THAT VOICE THAT IS FELT RATHER THAN HEARD."

—Boyd K. Packer

We receive answers
in many different ways.

IF ANY OF YOU LACK WISDOM, LET HIM ASK OF GOD, THAT GIVETH TO ALL MEN LIBERALLY, AND UPBRAIDETH NOT;
AND IT SHALL BE GIVEN HIM

Sometimes answers come from people who care about us, like parents or teachers.

Sometimes words will stand out to you when you are reading or listening to scriptures.

You may also get an urgent impression. It may be words you FEEL rather than HEAR.

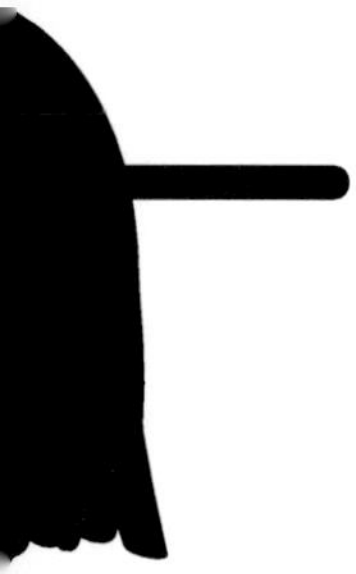

Sometimes we feel prompted
to say something or take action.

A prompting can be a strong
feeling, a warm feeling,
or a peaceful feeling.

Most revelation doesn't come
in just one burst. It comes
s l o w l y over time,
line
upon line.

"FOR BEHOLD, THUS SAITH THE LORD GOD: I WILL GIVE UNTO THE CHILDREN OF MEN LINE UPON LINE, PRECEPT UPON PRECEPT, HERE A LITTLE AND THERE A LITTLE; AND BLESSED ARE THOSE WHO HEARKEN UNTO MY PRECEPTS, AND LEND AN EAR UNTO MY COUNSEL, FOR THEY SHALL LEARN WISDOM; FOR UNTO HIM THAT RECEIVETH I WILL GIVE MORE."

—2 Nephi 28:30

We might have to be patient.

"WHEN IT COMES TO ETERNAL QUESTIONS, MATTERS OF THE SOUL, WE MUST BE MORE PATIENT… HEAVENLY ANSWERS—ETERNAL ANSWERS—ARE PRICELESS. RECEIVING THESE ANSWERS OFTEN REQUIRES SACRIFICE, WORK, AND PATIENCE."

—Dieter F. Uchtdorf

Sometimes the Lord expects us to decide for ourselves. Then we take our decision to Him and confirm that it is right.

"But, behold, I say unto you,
that you must study it out
in your mind; then you must ask me
if it be right, and if it is right I will
cause that your bosom shall burn
within you; therefore, you shall feel
that it is right. But if it be not right
you shall have no such feelings, but
you shall have a stupor of thought
that shall cause you to forget the
thing which is wrong."

—Doctrine and Covenants 9:8-9

Did you know we can also receive answers through dreams or visitations?

"THE VEIL BETWEEN HEAVEN AND EARTH USUALLY HIDES THE ANGELS FROM OUR SIGHT. YET...WE MAY EXPERIENCE UNMISTAKABLE CONTACT WITH THE ANGELS OF THE UNSEEN WORLD."

–Bruce C. Hafen

It's important to
remember promptings.
Try to write them down—
doing so can help
remind you to act on those
promptings too!

TODAY I felt INSPIRED to invite a friend to the park.
she told me it made her feel HAPPY!

We don't always get answers when we want or in a way we expect. Sometimes Heavenly Father's answer is "yes," some-times "no," and sometimes the answer is "wait."

Sometimes the answer we receive is no answer at all.

This experience can give us a chance to work things out on our own. We can strengthen our faith by going forward, using our own ability to think, and doing our best.

Heavenly Father knows what is best for us, and He will give us the things that will help us the most, because He loves us.

"IF YE … KNOW HOW TO GIVE GOOD GIFTS UNTO YOUR CHILDREN, HOW MUCH MORE SHALL YOUR FATHER WHICH IS IN HEAVEN GIVE GOOD THINGS TO THEM THAT ASK HIM?"

—Matthew 7:11

Receiving inspiration is another blessing and is often a broader experience—something that "enticeth" or invites us to do good.

"But behold,
that which is of God
inviteth and enticeth to do good
continually; wherefore,
every thing which inviteth
and enticeth to do good,
and to love God,
and to serve him,
is inspired of God."

—Moroni 7:13

Receiving revelation is a skill that usually requires practice and preparation.

As you practice and become more familiar with how Heavenly Father speaks to you through the Holy Ghost, you will also learn how to act on those promptings.

I AM
A CHILD
of
GOD
BOOK OF MORMON

“THERE IS NO LIMIT TO THE

REVELATIONS [WE] MAY RECEIVE."

—Bruce R. McConkie

Workbook

"AND NOW, HE IMPARTETH HIS WORD BY ANGELS UNTO MEN, YEA, NOT ONLY MEN BUT WOMEN ALSO. NOW THIS IS NOT ALL; LITTLE CHILDREN DO HAVE WORDS GIVEN UNTO THEM MANY TIMES, WHICH CONFOUND THE WISE AND THE LEARNED."

—Alma 32:23

ALL OF US HAVE QUESTIONS, AND QUESTIONS ARE GOOD!

Throughout our lives, we need to seek out truth. Heavenly Father loves each of us. He knows our names, our talents, our worries, and the longings of our hearts. He wants to hear from us and He wants to speak to us. That's why He gave us the Holy Ghost.

It is through the Gift of the Holy Ghost that we receive revelation, answers, inspiration, promptings, and comfort.

THE HOLY GHOST:

- Can warn us of danger or evil (Mosiah 23:1)
- Reveals truth to us (Moroni 10:5)
- Helps us remember things (John 14:26).
- Guides us in important decisions (2 Nephi 32:5).
- Inspires us (Luke 12:12).
- Helps us know and choose the right (D&C 11:12).
- Helps us understand things (D&C 6:15)

"AND IT SHALL COME TO PASS AFTERWARD, THAT I WILL POUR OUT MY SPIRIT UPON ALL FLESH; AND YOUR SONS AND YOUR DAUGHTERS SHALL PROPHESY, YOUR OLD MEN SHALL DREAM DREAMS, YOUR YOUNG MEN SHALL SEE VISIONS:AND ALSO UPON THE SERVANTS AND UPON THE HANDMAIDS IN THOSE DAYS WILL I POUR OUT MY SPIRIT."

- Joel 2:28–29

QUESTIONS FOR YOU AND YOUR FAMILY:

*Allow your children to answer the questions before giving your own answer or using any answers we have provided.

- What is the purpose of revelation?
  (To inform, comfort, uplift, warn, prophesy, testify etc.)

- What are some reasons we might want or need personal revelation from the Holy Ghost?

- What kinds of things does Heavenly Father expect us to decide on our own?

- How can you tell the difference between a prompting from the Holy Ghost and your own thoughts?

- Can you share an experience where you felt the Holy Ghost guiding you or answering a question or concern you had?

- Does Heavenly Father listen to our prayers even when we make mistakes? Why or why not?

"ANGELS SPEAK BY THE POWER OF THE HOLY GHOST; WHEREFORE, THEY SPEAK THE WORDS OF CHRIST. WHEREFORE, I SAID UNTO YOU, FEAST UPON THE WORDS OF CHRIST; FOR BEHOLD, THE WORDS OF CHRIST WILL TELL YOU ALL THINGS WHAT YE SHOULD DO.... FOR BEHOLD, AGAIN I SAY UNTO YOU THAT IF YE WILL ENTER IN BY THE WAY, AND RECEIVE THE HOLY GHOST, IT WILL SHOW UNTO YOU ALL THINGS WHAT YE SHOULD DO."

–2 Nephi 32:3, 5

PREPARING:

"... YIELDING TO EMOTIONS SUCH AS ANGER OR HURT OR DEFENSIVENESS WILL DRIVE AWAY THE HOLY GHOST. THOSE EMOTIONS MUST BE ELIMINATED, OR OUR CHANCE FOR RECEIVING REVELATION IS SLIGHT... A GOOD SENSE OF HUMOR HELPS REVELATION.... LOUD, INAPPROPRIATE LAUGHTER WILL OFFEND THE SPIRIT... CAREFUL, QUIET SPEECH WILL FAVOR THE RECEIPT OF REVELATION."
—Richard G. Scott

Spencer W. Kimball said, "God reveals himself to [people] who are prepared for such manifestations." Preparing to listen to the Holy Ghost and receive answers is a critical part of hearing and recognizing revelation. Having a desire to do what is right and a desire to know the truth is a must. Having a specific purpose helps you focus.

Reading scriptures helps us to be open to the Spirit and understand how God answers His people. Obedience (and repenting when we make mistakes), fasting, and talking with those who have experience with the issue we have questions about are also very helpful to receiving revelation.

Learn how the Holy Ghost talks to you! Understand what brings the Spirit of Revelation and the things that drive the Spirit away.

"BEHOLD, I SAY UNTO YOU THEY ARE MADE KNOWN UNTO ME BY THE HOLY SPIRIT OF GOD. BEHOLD, I HAVE FASTED AND PRAYED MANY DAYS THAT I MIGHT KNOW THESE THINGS OF MYSELF. AND NOW I DO KNOW OF MYSELF THAT THEY ARE TRUE; FOR THE LORD GOD HATH MADE THEM MANIFEST UNTO ME BY HIS HOLY SPIRIT; AND THIS IS THE SPIRIT OF REVELATION WHICH IS IN ME."
—Alma 5:46

QUESTIONS FOR YOU AND YOUR FAMILY:

- What are some ways we can prepare to receive revelation?
- How does keeping the commandments and our covenants help increase revelation?
- How can we increase our spiritual capacity to receive revelation?
- Why have many apostles and leaders said that morning time is sacred and a good time to pray to seek revelation?

ACTIVITIES:

"INSPIRATION COMES MORE EASILY IN PEACEFUL SETTINGS... REVERENCE INVITES REVELATION."
– Boyd K. Packer

Designate a place where you can receive personal revelation. Perhaps that is in your bedroom, in your closet, outside under a tree, etc. Think about something that you have questions about. Is there something you would like to gain a testimony about? Ponder on the topic. Study the scriptures and seek answers from your Heavenly Father. What can you do to make this a sacred experience?

FOR OLDER KIDS:

Discuss the following story and questions.

Sheri Dew related the following story: "In my early twenties, I faced a difficult decision and asked a friend for a priesthood blessing. He asked what the Lord had already told me, and I admitted that I could feel the presence of the Spirit but couldn't discern specific revelation. He then asked if I had ever asked the Lord to teach me what it felt like when He was speaking to me? I hadn't. But that night, I began to ask the Lord to teach me the language of revelation."

- **How can you follow Sister Dew's example to learn the language of revelation?**
- **What steps can you take?**
- **Where can you learn the language of revelation?**
- **Do you know anyone who already knows the language of revelation?**
- **Is the language of revelation the same for each person?**

ASKING:

"None of us are entitled to revelation without effort on our part. Answers from God don't just magically appear. If we want to grow spiritually, the Lord expects us to ask questions and seek answers." —Sheri Dew

Talking with our Heavenly Father, seeking His guidance, and asking Him questions are essential if we are to grow our testimony and discover truth. He has promised that if we knock, it shall be opened to us. However, there is a right way to ask. We must ask in faith, meaning that we believe that God loves us and will answer us. We must also ask with an honest heart, meaning that we are asking because we really want to know the answer so that we can make a good choice and do what is right.

"One of the great lessons that each of us needs to learn is to ask. Why does the Lord want us to pray to Him and to ask? Because that is how revelation is received." —Richard G. Scott

QUESTIONS FOR YOU AND YOUR FAMILY:

- What does "knock and it shall be opened unto you" mean?
- How can we be sincere and humble in our questions to Heavenly Father?
- What does it mean to ask with "real intent"?

- What does it mean to "ask in faith, nothing wavering" (James 1:6)?
- Does this mean we have to have perfect faith to ask questions of the Lord?
- What can we do if we don't even know what questions we want to ask?
- If we don't feel like we have gotten an answer is it okay to ask Heavenly Father again?

ACTIVITIES:

PATTERNS

The prophet Joseph Smith set a pattern for us to follow in resolving our questions: "If any of you lack wisdom let him ask of God …" Read the story of the First Vision. Think about the steps Joseph took in order to find truth. Where did he go to pray and why? What steps can you take in order to receive revelation?

Read the talk, "Revelation for the Church, Revelation for Our Lives," given by President Russell M. Nelson. He discusses the pattern he and the Quorum of the Twelve Apostles follow when receiving revelation for the Church. Where do they go to pray to get answers? Why must the Spirit be present in their meetings? Why does he say "in our meetings, the majority never rules"?

LISTENING AND GETTING ANSWERS:

"AND HE SAID, GO FORTH, AND STAND UPON THE MOUNT BEFORE THE LORD. AND, BEHOLD, THE LORD PASSED BY, AND A GREAT AND STRONG WIND RENT THE MOUNTAINS, AND BRAKE IN PIECES THE ROCKS BEFORE THE LORD; BUT THE LORD WAS NOT IN THE WIND: AND AFTER THE WIND AN EARTHQUAKE; BUT THE LORD WAS NOT IN THE EARTHQUAKE: AND AFTER THE EARTHQUAKE A FIRE; BUT THE LORD WAS NOT IN THE FIRE: AND AFTER THE FIRE A STILL SMALL VOICE." —1 Kings 19: 11–12

We receive revelation and answers to questions in many different ways. Sometimes we don't realize that we are being prompted until later. Richard G. Scott taught two ways we can know that we have been answered. He said that you can know that a prompting or feeling is from God if it "produces peace in your heart AND a quiet, warm feeling."

REVELATION CAN BE:

- Words you feel rather than hear in your heart and your mind
- A prompting or sacred feeling
- A voice
- A dream
- A visitation
- Words that stand out to you or a warm feeling during your scripture study—this is the Holy Ghost testifying of their truthfulness

THE HOLY GHOST CAN:

- **Bring something to your remembrance**
- **Make words a teacher or parent says stand out to you so strongly that you cannot deny they are important and meant for you**

Please understand there is not one, right way to receive revelation. All of us, especially kids, are in training to understand revelation and hear God speak to us. If you feel like you are not getting an answer, rely on the word of God found in the scriptures and use your best judgement.

When you receive revelation, don't just get up and move on to the next activity. Ponder what you have heard and felt. If possible write down the feelings and impressions you receive.

"...I prayed, reviewing with the Lord what I thought I had been taught by the Spirit. When a feeling of peace came, I thanked Him for the guidance given. I was then impressed to ask, "Was there yet more to be given?" I received further impressions, and the process of writing down the impressions, pondering, and praying for confirmation was repeated. Again I was prompted to ask, "Is there more I should know?" And there was." **–Richard G. Scott**

QUESTIONS FOR YOU AND YOUR FAMILY:

- Most revelation comes in small increments, a bit at a time. Even though Joseph Smith's first vision of God the Father and Jesus Christ was glorious, it was still just the beginning. After this vision was Joseph immediately given the golden plates and asked to translate? How long did he have to wait and how much spiritual tutoring took place before he was ready to translate the Book of Mormon and establish the Church of Jesus Christ of Latter-day Saints?

- How can we be more patient in learning and preparing to receive answers?

- What does the Holy Ghost sounds like?

"AND IT CAME TO PASS WHEN THEY HEARD THIS VOICE, AND BEHELD THAT IT WAS NOT A VOICE OF THUNDER, NEITHER WAS IT A VOICE OF A GREAT TUMULTUOUS NOISE, BUT BEHOLD, IT WAS A STILL VOICE OF PERFECT MILDNESS, AS IF IT HAD BEEN A WHISPER, AND IT DID PIERCE EVEN TO THE VERY SOUL—" – Helaman 5:30

- How can we recognize when the Holy Ghost is communicating to us? Elder David R. Bednar taught, "I think we overcomplicate this.... All good emanates from Christ, so if you have a thought to do something good, it's prompted by the Holy Ghost.... If it invites and entices to do good, it comes from Christ, and we ought to do it."

"BUT BEHOLD, THAT WHICH IS OF GOD INVITETH AND ENTICETH TO DO GOOD CONTINUALLY; WHEREFORE, EVERY THING WHICH INVITETH AND ENTICETH TO DO GOOD, AND TO LOVE GOD, AND TO SERVE HIM, IS INSPIRED OF GOD." –Moroni 7:13

- How can we hear the Holy Ghost more often and more clearly?
- What are some things that make it difficult to hear or feel the Holy Ghost communicating to us?
- Sometimes we have emergencies and we need an answer immediately, like when trying to avoid an accident or when facing peer pressure. Do we need to sit down and search the scriptures at such a time? (No, we can ask for the Lord's guidance at any time.)

ACTIVITIES:

Read and discuss the following story:

"Susan was a wonderful seamstress [and] President Kimball lived in [her] ward. One Sunday, Susan noticed that he had a new suit. Her father had recently returned from a trip to New York and had brought her some exquisite silk fabric. Susan thought that fabric would make a handsome tie to go with President Kimball's new suit. So on Monday she made the tie. She wrapped it in tissue paper and walked up the block to President Kimball's home. On her way to the front door, she suddenly stopped and thought, 'Who am I to make a tie for the prophet? He probably has plenty of them.' Deciding she had made a mistake, she turned to leave. Just then Sister Kimball opened the front door and said, 'Oh, Susan!' Stumbling all over herself, Susan said, 'I saw President Kimball in his new suit on Sunday. Dad just brought me some silk from New York ... and so I made him a tie.'

Before Susan could continue, Sister Kimball stopped her, took hold of her shoulders, and said: 'Susan, never suppress a generous thought.'"

- What did Sister Kimball mean by "never suppress a generous thought"?

  What are some examples of kind, thoughtful things that the Spirit may prompt us to do?

- Have you ever ignored a generous thought?

- Who is someone in your life that may need your kindness or generosity?

- Does "never suppress a generous thought" mean that you never say "no" to helping others? Might there be times where the generous thing to do is to not help?

Read Doctrine and Covenants 9 where Oliver Cowdery received revelation about his inability to translate the Book of Mormon. Why couldn't Oliver translate the plates? What did he neglect to do? What decisions in our lives require us to "study it out," make a decision, and then ask Heavenly Father "if it be right?" What will we feel if our decision is right?

In a journal, write down what you have recently learned during your prayers or while being inspired in some other way. If you are comfortable, share what you have learned with your family.

ACTING UPON PERSONAL REVELATION

"THE LORD WILL TEACH US DIRECTLY AS MUCH TRUTH AS WE ARE WORTHY AND WILLING TO LEARN."
—Sheri Dew

Heavenly Father expects us to ACT. If we expect Heavenly Father to guide us and give us further revelation and truth then we need to act upon the revelation He gives. Whether it is a small feeling of inspiration or a strong, direct prompting, we must follow His counsel and His commands.

Sometimes He expects us to act in faith, even when we don't feel like we have gotten all the answers we think we need. Sometimes we may feel like we only have a couple of pieces to a large puzzle. Heavenly Father still expects us to act. Nephi was commanded to get the gold plates from Laban even though he had not received a plan of action from God. Queen Esther was brave enough to approach her husband the king in order to save her people even though she had no assurance that her husband would not be offended and order her death.

God just expects us to do our best!

THE WITNESS OF THE HOLY GHOST MAKES AN IMPRESSION ON THE SOUL THAT IS MORE SIGNIFICANT THAN ANYTHING WE CAN SEE OR HEAR. THROUGH SUCH REVELATIONS, WE WILL RECEIVE LASTING STRENGTH TO STAY TRUE TO THE GOSPEL AND HELP OTHERS DO THE SAME. —True to the Faith

DISCUSSION QUESTIONS:

Sometimes we don't have all the information or we may feel like we haven't yet received revelation. Does this mean that we don't have to act? Does Heavenly Father expect us to move forward with big or small decisions even if we don't feel that we have received revelation?

- President Russell M. Nelson said, "Revelation comes at the frontier of knowledge and experience." What does this mean?
- What happens if I ignore a prompting from the Holy Ghost?
- Are our prayers always answered?

DEEPER QUESTIONS:

- What can we do if we feel like our prayers are not being answered?
- Have you ever prayed for something and not recognized the answer to your prayer until later?
- Have you ever prayed to know how the Lord feels about you? Try it!
- Imagine that God is sitting next to you. What would He say?
  What would He want to reveal to you?
- When we don't feel like we are being answered, how should we proceed?

"We have learned
to treasure the spiritual gems
that are revealed through
repetition. Repetition is
a vehicle through which the
Holy Ghost can
enlighten our minds,
influence our hearts,
and enlarge
our understanding."

—David A. Bednar

GLOSSARY:

Capacity: Your ability to do something or the amount something can hold.

Faith: Faith is to hope for things which are not seen, but which are true (Hebrews 11:1; Alma 32:21), and must be centered in Jesus Christ in order to produce salvation.

Holy Ghost: The third member of the Godhead and a personage of Spirit. "The Holy Ghost is a revelator," said Joseph Smith, and "no man can receive the Holy Ghost without receiving revelations" (HC 6:58). By the power of the Holy Ghost a person receives a testimony of Jesus Christ and of His work and the work of His servants upon the earth. The gift of the Holy Ghost, received only after baptism and confirmation, is the right to have, whenever one is worthy, the companionship of the Holy Ghost.

Impression: Words you feel rather than hear.

Inspiration: Divine guidance given to man by God. Inspiration often comes by the Spirit in a variety of ways to the mind or heart of a person.

Personal Revelation: An active process in which a person seeks to find truth and knowledge. The revelation a person receives can help with specific personal needs, responsibilities, and questions. It can also build and strengthen an individual's testimony. Every person may receive personal revelation for their own benefit.

Ponder: To think about something carefully, usually before making a decision or reaching a conclusion.

Priesthood Blessing: A process by which one or more men ordained to the Melchizedek Priesthood lay hands on the head of someone in need of direction or healing from God. Through the inspiration of the Holy Ghost, the speaker receives the words of the blessing from the Lord and pronounces them upon the person receiving the blessing.

Prompting: A strong, warm feeling or a peaceful feeling. It is also described as a sacred feeling or words in your mind that entice you to do good. It can also be a command.

Prophet: A leader who is called by God to be His mouthpiece on the earth and to conduct the affairs of the Church according to the will and revelation of the Lord.

Real Intent: In relation to prayer and revelation, it is being sincere, expecting an answer, and having the determination to do what is right and act on the revelation given. Russell M. Nelson Nelson said, 'real intent' means that one really intends to follow the divine direction given."

Revelation: Communication from God to His children through the whisperings of the Holy Ghost or by other means, such as visions, dreams, or visitations.

Reverence: A deep feeling of respect; to honor. When a person is reverent, she may speak quietly, or not talk at all so that the Spirit may be present and so she can hear the promptings of the Holy Ghost.

WORKS CITED

"8 Important Questions Youth Asked Elder Bednar at Yesterday's Worldwide Event." LDS Living. June 18, 2016. Accessed November 15, 2019. http://www.ldsliving.com/8-Important-Questions-Youth-Asked-Elder-Bednar-at-Yesterday-s-Worldwide-Event/s/78901.

Beck, Julie B. "'And upon the Handmaids in Those Days Will I Pour Out My Spirit.'" Accessed March 10, 2019. https://www.lds.org/general-conference/2010/04/and-upon-the-handmaids-in-those-days-will-i-pour-out-my-spirit?lang=eng.

Bednar, David A. "The Spirit of Revelation." Accessed February 1, 2019. https://www.lds.org/general-conference/2011/04/the-spirit-of-revelation?lang=eng.

Craig, Michelle D. "Divine Discontent." Accessed March 18, 2019. https://www.lds.org/general-conference/2018/10/divine-discontent?lang=eng.

Dew, Sheri. "Will You Engage in the Wrestle?" BYU–Idaho Devotional. Accessed January 4, 2019. https://www.byui.edu/devotionals/sheri-dew.

Eyring, Henry B. "Continuing Revelation." Accessed March 1, 2019. https://www.lds.org/general-conference/2014/10/continuing-revelation?lang=eng.

"Face to Face with Elder and Sister Bednar." Youth Activities. Accessed December 26, 2018. https://www.lds.org/youth/activities/spiritual-strength/scriptures-and-prophets/face-to-face-with-elder-and-sister-bednar?lang=eng.

"Faith." Bible Dictionary. Accessed March 17, 2019. https://www.lds.org/scriptures/bd/faith?lang=eng&letter=F.

Faust, James E. "Communion with the Holy Spirit." Accessed February 13, 2019. https://www.lds.org/study/liahona/2002/03/communion-with-the-holy-spirit?lang=eng.

Hafen, Bruce C. When Do the Angels Come? Accessed March 29, 2019. https://www.lds.org/study/ensign/1992/04/when-do-the-angels-come?lang=eng.

"Heavenly Father Answers Our Prayers." Family Home Evening Resource Book. Lesson Seven. Accessed January 20, 2019. https://www.lds.org/manual/family-home-evening-resource-book/family-home-evening-lessons/lesson-seven-heavenly-father-answers-our-prayers?lang=eng.

"Holy Ghost." Bible Dictionary. Accessed March 1, 2019. https://www.lds.org/scriptures/bd/holy-ghost.

"Inspiration, Inspire." Guide to the Scriptures. Accessed March 2, 2019. https://www.lds.org/scriptures/gs/inspiration-inspire.

Kendrick, L. Lionel. "Personal Revelation." BYU Speeches. Accessed January 9, 2019. https://speeches.byu.edu/talks/l-lionel-kendrick_personal-revelation/.

"Learning to Recognize the Spirit." Family Home Evening Resource Book. Lesson Fifteen. Accessed November 22, 2019. https://www.lds.org/manual/family-home-evening-resource-book/family-home-evening-lessons/lesson-fifteen-learning-to-recognize-the-spirit?lang=eng.

Lund, Gerald N. Why Isn't God Answering Me?Salt Lake City, Utah: Deseret Book, 2018.

Maxwell, Neal A. "Meek and Lowly." BYU Speeches. Accessed January 5, 2019. https://speeches.byu.edu/talks/neal-a-maxwell_meek-lowly/.

Nelson, Russell M. "Ask, Seek, Knock." Accessed November 30, 2018. https://www.lds.org/general-conference/2009/10/ask-seek-knock?lang=eng.

Nelson, Russell M. "Revelation for the Church, Revelation for Our Lives." By President Russell M. Nelson. Accessed January 28, 2019. https://www.lds.org/general-conference/2018/04/revelation-for-the-church-revelation-for-our-lives?lang=eng.

Oaks, Dallin H. "Eight Ways God Can Speak to You." Accessed March 2, 2019. https://www.lds.org/study/new-era/2004/09/eight-ways-god-can-speak-to-you?lang=eng.

Packer, Boyd K. "Counsel to Youth." Accessed December 16, 2018. https://www.lds.org/study/ensign/2011/11/saturday-morning-session/counsel-to-youth?lang=eng.

Packer, Boyd K. "Reverence Invites Revelation." Accessed March 23, 2019. https://www.lds.org/general-conference/1991/10/reverence-invites-revelation?lang=eng.

Parkin, Bonnie D. "Personal Ministry: Sacred and Precious." BYU Speeches. Accessed March 16, 2019. https://speeches.byu.edu/talks/bonnie-d-parkin_personal-ministry-sacred-precious/.

Pearce, Virginia H. "Prayer: A Small and Simple Thing." BYU Women's Conference, 2011. Accessed March 18, 2019. https://womensconference.byu.edu/sites/womensconference.ce.byu.edu/files/virginia_pearce.pdf.

"Ponder | Definition of Ponder in English by Oxford Dictionaries." Oxford Dictionaries | English. Accessed March 2, 2019. https://en.oxforddictionaries.com/definition/ponder.

"Repeat Over Again ... the Same Things as Before." BYU–Idaho Devotionals. Accessed February 11, 2019. http://www.byui.edu/devotionals/elder-david-a-bednar.

"Revelation." True to the Faith. Accessed March 2, 2019. https://www.lds.org/manual/true-to-the-faith/revelation?lang=eng.

"Revelation." Bible Dictionary. Accessed February 28, 2019. https://www.lds.org/scriptures/bd/revelation?lang=eng.

Scott, Richard G. "To Acquire Spiritual Guidance." Richard G. Scott. Accessed March 29, 2019. https://www.lds.org/general-conference/2009/10/to-acquire-spiritual-guidance?lang=eng.

Scott, Richard G. "How to Obtain Revelation and Inspiration for Your Personal Life." Accessed November 13, 2018. https://www.lds.org/general-conference/2012/04/how-to-obtain-revelation-and-inspiration-for-your-personal-life?lang=eng.

Uchtdorf, Dieter F. Your Adventure through Mortality. Accessed March 16, 2019. https://www.lds.org/study/ensign/2019/03/your-adventure-through-mortality?lang=eng.

Worthen, Kevin J. "Receiving Revelation." BYU Speeches. Accessed February 12, 2019. https://speeches.byu.edu/talks/kevin-j-worthen_receiving-revelation/.

ABOUT THE AUTHOR:

Dina Alexander is the founder and CEO of Educate and Empower Kids (educateempowerkids.org), an organization dedicated to strengthening families by teaching digital citizenship, media literacy, and healthy sexuality education—including education about the dangers of online porn.

In 2018, President Russell M. Nelson said, "In coming days, it will not be possible to survive spiritually without the guiding, directing, comforting, and constant influence of the Holy Ghost.... If we are to have any hope of sifting through the myriad of voices and the philosophies of men that attack truth, we must learn to receive revelation." With these words, Dina knew she needed to do something to help her own children and other kids understand the great potential they have to receive and understand personal revelation. After much prayer and contemplation, This is the Spirit of Revelation began to take shape.

Prior to writing this, her first Latter-day Saint children's book, Dina wrote Petra's Power to See: A Media Literacy Adventure and Noah's New Phone: A Story About Using Technology for Good, and co-wrote the Messages About Me: A Journey to Healthy Body Image books for boys and girls.

For adults, she and her team created How to Talk to Your Kids About Pornography, 30 Days to a Stronger Child, and 30 Days of Sex Talks: Empowering Your Child with a Knowledge of Sexual Intimacy for Kids Ages 3–7, 8–11, and 12+. She received her master's degree in recreation therapy from the University of Utah and her bachelors from Brigham Young University. Dina has taught in various capacities for over twenty years, including marriage enhancement, art for small children, and group fitness. She has also worked with teenage girls in a residential treatment setting, adults with drug addictions, and special needs children. She and her family live in the Rio Rancho Stake in New Mexico.

**IF YOU ENJOYED THIS BOOK,
PLEASE LEAVE A POSITIVE REVIEW ON AMAZON.COM**

For great resources and information, follow us on Instagram:
@dina_empower_ldskids

Subscribe to our website for exclusive offers and information at:
www.empowerlatterdaysaintkids.org

Made in the
USA
Monee, IL

15615442R00050